A UNIQUE CREATION OF DON BOSCO

TOWARDS A COMPREHENSION OF THE VOCATION OF THE SALESIAN BROTHERS

BOSCO EKKA | SDB

Copyright © Bosco Ekka, Sdb
All Rights Reserved.

Contents

Preface

There are two types of vocations in man's religious life: brothers and priests. In the monastic life, the two types of calling are more obvious. There is a distinction between these two types of religious call.

When referring to a priest, the writer might state that he is highly powerful or well-known among Catholics and the broader public. While the brothers' appeal to Catholics and the general public is not yet and not particularly understood, this is due to the fact that they seldom witness and experience personally their work. One paradigm or ideal for parents whose children join seminary study is that their son will one day become a priest. There is no other.

The author discusses the figure of a brother's call in this book: The first vocation of a religious Brother in the Church is the development of the consecration conferred by the Sacraments of Baptism and Faith. the world, and the Church's own mission to witness and proclaim the Gospel. And, according to Lumen Gentium art. 43 of The Second Vatican Council, "this state of life finds its place in the organisation of the Ecclesiastical Hierarchy." This vocation's position is more than merely a bridge between the priestly and lay vocations. This call is to be considered as a distinctive vocation for Christians, allowing them to experience unique grace within the Church and contributing to the Church's rescue mission in various ways."

Second, what is the Salesian Brother's vocation? According to General Chapter 21 (GC21), the Salesian Coadjutor (now Salesian Brother - SB) is a baptised person called by God to commit himself completely to Him in Christ, to serve Him as a "lay religious" in the Salesian Congregation for Young People. Don Bosco promotes holistic Christian education for young people, particularly the poorest, via it and in collaboration with the Salesian priest. The community then educates about Salesian Brothers, who "cross the realm of consecration with the hosts of the state" by living the lay state as a consecrated person. "The presence of Salesian Brothers improves the community's apostolic activities." It continuously reminds the clerical sector of the ideals inherent in lay religious vocations and invites them to active partnership with lay people. It also recalls to the Salesian priests a vision of an apostolic objective and ideal that is complicated in its actuality, since it extends beyond formal priestly and catechetical work."

Third, what is the Salesian Brother's position in the Salesian Congregation? The following are the three roles that the author might play: First, by virtue of his consecrated existence, he performs ministerial tasks; second, as a Salesian, the Brother is first and foremost a "educational," dedicating himself by vow to the total growth of the young and ordinary people. He performs cultural, professional, social, and financial obligations in addition to catechetical, liturgical, and missionary duties; in other words, he is involved in "every sector of education and pastoral action." Because, as a religious, he is profoundly involved in pastoral ministry, giving a specific expression to his baptismal priesthood; and third, his lay situation and experience, combined with a truly Salesian heart, bring him particularly "near... to the young and to the reality of working life." His Salesian heart is based in the transcendence he experiences in temporal realities into which he injects the Gospel's tremendous force. This allows him to operate in a secular setting with a mindset that is both "technical" and "pastoral," which is very valuable to the community.

Through the book, the author hopes to assist people or catholics in general, and especially young people and candidates in their initial formation, in comprehending and appreciating God's call, in comprehending and appreciating the vocation of Salesian Brother, in comprehending and appreciating the Salesian Brothers' deep reflection, in comprehending and appreciating the Salesian Brothers' place and role in the Salesian Congregation, in comprehending and appreciating the Salesian Brothers' challenge and joy as Salesian Brothers.

They can use it to study, learn about, and develop an appreciation for the Salesian Brother vocation. Finally, some of them may discover or rediscover their vocation and voluntarily and deliberately choose to become a Salesian Brother.

Acknowledgements

First and foremost, I'd want to thank God for the light of His inspiration that has supported me throughout the process of completing this book. This whole educational quest was only made possible by His grace and kindness.

Thank you to the Don Bosco Center of Studies and all of my lecturers for teaching me that there is indescribable delight in learning about God and real satisfaction in serving the Lord.

Thank you to my Salesian Brothers and Priests in those communities for your support and excellent example for me and my vocation, particularly in this trip to accomplish this project paper with you. Your devotion to God has always been a source of tremendous inspiration to me. To the young people, I am grateful for the opportunity to have met and will meet everyone of you in my life as part of the task to which I have been assigned. Thank you very much.

Blessed Artemi de Zatti, a Salesian Brother who influenced me. I realised that his life as a Salesian Brother was so simple, unique, good, and committed to helping those in need. I was impressed by his biography. His life was completely dedicated to God and to those in need, particularly the ill. He never said no to assisting them. He was always willing to assist, even late at night. That, he thought, was a summons. He also spent time with his community, including prayer, leisure, and labour. His life had an impact on me, and I aspired to be like him. Despite the fact that I had never met him, his biography made me believe he was still alive. He was both human and divine.

Finally, thank you to St. John Bosco and the Salesians Saints for their inspiration and prayers in completing this endeavour. I will be eternally thankful for what you have taught us, and I will give my life for the cause of your people. You have motivated me to view myself through the eyes of the Father.

CHAPTER ONE

Introduction

When individuals encounter a religious Brother, they often ask these questions: "How do you define a religious Brother?" "How do they make a living?" "What is the point of being a religious brother?" "Why would you want to be a religious brother rather than a priest?" "Why are you not a priest?" "Is it possible for a brother to become a priest?" plus a slew of additional inquiries!

We sometimes make the wrong decisions about what it means to be a Salesian Brother. Someone might think that because a Salesian Brother doesn't go to school like his clerical comrades, he doesn't need to be good at his own trade and education. This isn't true. The Salesian Brother pursues his calling by becoming an educator for young people in their own settings. But if you look more closely at the meaning of a call, it turns out that it's very different from what you think. People, in general, can't fully understand the difference. Why? In general, the call to brotherhood is very rare. The call to priesthood is more common, but recently there has been a drop in vocations to the priesthood.

The writer, on the other hand, thinks that becoming a brother is both a call and a choice. It's not an option or choice that can be changed or forced by anyone else. The thing about freedom is very important. It's also possible to become a brother because you have seen how other brothers have lived and worked as a witness, either by living with them or by reading their biographical books. These inspirational stories make the brother want to go for the option with a smile on his face.

There are a lot of official Church documents or sources that explain the position and identity of brothers who have been called to live a consecrated life in the Church. It says in Perfectae Caritatis, chapter 10, that God is always good to us.

> *"Religious life of lay members, for men and women, is a status of practicing the complete gospel counsels. Thus the Sacred Council greatly appreciates it, as so meritorious to the pastoral duties of the Church, through the education of the youth, the care of the sick, and the other ministries. The Council affirms its members in their vocation, and encourages them to adapt their lives to the demands of the present times.[1]"*

In addition, we can also find *Lumen Gentium* art. 43, that "This status of life has its place in the structure of the ecclesiastical hierarchy. The status of this vocation is not a middle way between the vocation of the priest and the laity. This call should be regarded as a special vocation for Christians, enabling them to enjoy special grace within the Church, and in each way contributing to the Church's rescue mission."[2] This statement has existed in *The Code of Canon Law*, canon 588 §1. For this reason, the "lay consecration" of both men and women constitutes a state which in its profession of the evangelical counsels is complete in itself. Consequently, both for the individual and for the Church, it has a value in itself, apart from the sacred ministry."[3]

In the book *Iman Katolik*, KWI is written, Brothers and Sisters are not members of the hierarchy, and all the nuns do not belong to the hierarchy. It's just that there are monks who are ordained priests. They are at the same time members of the monastic and auxiliary group of the bishop, but living in a monastic way is not an ecclesiastical function, but a feature of life. Therefore, the Second Vatican Council teaches, even though the status embodied by the exposition of gospel counsels, excludes them from the hierarchical order of the Church, but also cannot be divorced from the life and purity of the Church, for monastic life evolves from the life of the Church itself, even counsel The Gospel is based on God's word and example.[4]

Then our congregation teaches about Salesian brothers that the Salesian Brother "combines in himself the gifts of consecration with those of the lay state": he lives the lay state as a consecrated person. We read:

The presence of the Salesian Brother enriches the apostolic activity of the community. It reminds the clerical section of the values inherent in the lay religious vocation and recalls them constantly to an active collaboration with laypeople. It also recalls to the Salesian priests the vision of an apostolic goal and ideal that is complex in its reality, because it goes beyond priestly and catechetical activity in the strict sense." The Salesian Brother has a significant role to play, especially in certain contexts where the priest is seen as a sacred or cultic figure. By his consecrated life he proclaims the presence of God in daily life, and the importance of becoming disciples before being teachers, and bears witness to a convinced life of faith not tied to functional or ministerial duties.[5]

The writer had an experience as a brother. When he entered the Salesian community, he saw two kinds of Salesian vocation, priests and brothers, that supported each other. At that time, there were three brothers present among us in our community. Priests or brothers were happy and did many things together, except when the priest was the only one to say Mass. The brothers spent their time in the workshop (training centre) with the young people and students. He found that Salesian Brother's vocation was in demand.

So, in the novitiate, he wrote a letter asking to become a Salesian Brother. His Novice Master found out his choice to be a Salesian Brother, he then said, "if one day, a younger priest becomes a rector, would you obey him?" "Yes, he replied, because Don Bosco said we should obey to our rector as he is." Then he was smiling at him. On another day, the novice master approached him and said that he did not believe that his choice was decided as yet. Until he made his perpetual profession, the novice master then supported his vocation. Finally, he made it and he prayed that God protects and guide him until the end.

And after he became a Salesian Brother (with temporary vows) when he visited his family for the first time, they asked him about his vocation. Would he someday be a priest? And he replied that he is a brother and will be a Brother. Some of his brothers did not understand it. In his place, when one enters the seminary, it means he will become a priest. But he explained to them that in a Salesian family we are the same, either brother or priest. His aunt said, "It is ok, as long as he is happy, and enjoys his vocation!" On hearing his aunt's comment, he felt it was like God's voice and he was happy to hear it.

[1] Austin Flannery, O.P. (General Editor), Vatican Council II, *Perfectae Caritatis*, New Revised Edition (Pasay City - Philippines: Paulines Publishing House, 2007), 616.

[2] *Ibid., Lumen Gentium*, 403.

[3] John Paul II, *Vita Consacrata* (Pasay City - Philippines: Paulines Publishing House, 2015), 82.

[4] Konferensi Waligereja Indonesia, *Iman Katolik* (Indonesia: Kanisius and Obor, 1996), 375.

[5] Formation of Salesians of Don Bosco: Principles and Norms, Ratio Fundamentalis Institutions et Studiorum, Third Editionn (Rome, 2009), 49-50.

Related Literature

In this book the writer would like to make use of all possible methods in order to get clear and if possible first-hand information regarding the situation of formation to the Brother's vocation in the Church especially in the delegation of Indonesia. Hence, the overall method that will be used for this book will be the pastoral spiral, i.e., the "See- Judge-Act" method. See Step – This step will be used in Chapter Two. In this chapter, the writer observes the Salesian Brother's vocation in the real identity of the Salesian Brother. The "Judge Step"

As we progress from chapter to chapter, the following methods prove themselves helpful: (1) The theological interpretative methodology through Don Bosco Center of Studies' library research. By a careful reading of the theme dealt with already Salesians of Don Bosco writings documents; (2) Reflections on personal experiences: the few years of formative experiences in the brotherhood of the writer.

Constitutions of The Society of St Francis de Sales, Third edition. India, 2009.

In this Holy Book of our Congregation, article 22 says that each one of us is called by God to form part of the Salesian Society. Because of this God gives him personal gifts, and by faithful correspondence, he finds his way to complete fulfilment in Christ.

And in article 96, it says that He (God) calls us to live out in the Church our founder's project as apostles of the young. We respond to this call by committing ourselves to an adequate ongoing formation, for which the Lord daily gives us his grace.

From this book, we can know that all vocations in Salesian Society, priests or brothers, are from God. God is the initiator to call those people who will continue his mission for this time and need. This book will be used by the writer in chapters two, three and four of this project paper.

The Salesian Brother: History, Identity Vocational Apostolate and Formation. Rome, 1989.

This book explains clearly the Salesian Brother. The word for the calling of the Salesian Brothers as Salesian Coadjutors was the first call in the thought of Don Bosco, the Founder. This book has four chapters and speaks about the Salesian Brother. Starting from the History, vocational Identity of the Salesian Brother, the vocation of the Salesian Brother in Salesian Pastoral works for vocations and outlines the formation of the Salesian Brother. From this book, we can know the deep meaning of the Salesian brother which the writer will explain in chapters one, two and four of this project paper.

Acts World Congress of The Salesian Brother. Rome, 1975.

There are many things that speak about the Salesian Brother in that Congress but here I stress the point of "some practical needs in the formation of the Brother" on pages 327 till 341. These points remind the writer about those people who have the task to take care of formation houses, initial formation to form those candidates following the formation steps. And the last part of this book explains again the significance of the Identity of the Salesian Brother, prospects for the apostolic work of the Salesian Brother, the formation of the Salesian Brother, and vocation proposals for the youth of present-day society. From these resources, the writer will explain this in chapters one, two and four of this project paper.

Fr. Jose Carbonell Llopis, SDB: Perintis Salesian di Indonesia. Jakarta, 2010.

As a whole, this book actually is a biography of one Salesian Missionary Priest, Fr Carbonell, SDB as a gift for his 80th Birthday celebration. The reporter wrote this book in the way of interviewers and outlines the history of the priest in his mission. Fr Carbonell is the Salesian pioneer in Indonesia with a great spirit and hard work to foster the Salesian work and vocation. This source is used by the writer in chapter three.

East Asia Oceania Salesian Brothers' Congress. Hua Hin, Thailand 18- 23 August 2013.

This section reflects on the situation of the Salesian Brothers in the Salesian Congregation made in their reflection on the life of Salesian Brothers today. This congress is the important congress in our region, Asia Oceania Salesian Brothers. This book describes our situation and is connected to our daily life, as Salesian Brothers. This source will be used by the writer in chapter four of this book.

Vita Consecrata: Apostolic Exhortation of His Holiness John Paul II. Pasay City - Philippines: Paulines Publishing House, 2015. Page 82.

Pope John Paul II, in his Apostolic Exhortation *Vita Consecrata* no. 60 says that according to the traditional doctrine of the Church, the consecrated life by its nature is neither lay nor clerical. This statement has existed in *The Code of Canon Law*, canon 588 §1. For this reason, the "lay consecration" of both men and women constitutes a state that in its profession of the evangelical counsels is complete in itself. Consequently, both for the individual and for the Church, it is a value in itself, apart from the sacred ministry. This quote will be used by the writer in chapter two of this project paper about the Church document for Lay Religious.

Acts of the General Council of the Salesian Society of St John Bosco, year XCIII, may-august 2012, N. 413

In the Letter of the Rector Major, Fr Pascual Chavez Villanueva said that as a Council we examined the Challenges which are facing us in the congregation. In number two He explained "Salesian Life and Mission in Today's Global Context". There are some challenges: cultural, ecclesial, institutional, personal and young people. And in number three he mentioned "The Radical Approach of the Gospel in Salesian Consecrated Life". He wrote on some points: vocation as God's call and vocation to the Salesian Consecrated life which places us as disciples and apostles of the Lord Jesus in the footsteps of Don Bosco's, spiritual experience: disciples of Christ and seekers of God, in fraternal life: in Fraternal communities, mission: sent to the young, work and temperance, are the two requirements: processes to be set in motion, mindset to be changed and structures to be changed. This part, the writer will put in chapter four of this project paper.

Formation of Salesians of Don Bosco: Principles and Norms, Ratio Fundamentalis Institutionis et Studiorum, Third Editionn. Rome, 2009, pp 49-50.

The Salesian Brother "combines in himself the gifts of consecration with those of the lay state": he lives in the lay state as a consecrated person. "The presence of the Salesian Brother enriches the apostolic activity of the community. It reminds the priest members of the values inherent in the lay religious vocation and recalls them constantly to an active collaboration with laypeople. It also recalls to the Salesian priests the vision of an apostolic goal and ideal that is complex in its reality, because it goes beyond priestly and catechetical activity in the strict sense". He has a significant role to play, especially in a certain context where the priest is seen as a sacred or cultic figure. By his consecrated life he proclaims the presence of God in daily life, the importance of becoming disciples before being teachers, and bears witness to a convinced life of faith not tied to functional or ministerial duties. From this source, the writer will explain in chapters one, two and four in this book.

Iman Katolik: Buku Informasi dan Referensi, Konferensi Waligereja Indonesia. Indonesia: Kanisius and Obor, 1996.

As a whole, this book explains the religious people. There it is written, Brothers and Sisters are not members of the hierarchy, and all the nuns do not belong to the hierarchy. It's just that there are monks who are ordained priests. They are at the same time members of the monastic and auxiliary group of the bishop, but living in a monastic way is not an ecclesiastical function, but a feature of life. Therefore, the *Second Vatican Council* teaches, even though the status embodied by the exposition of gospel counsels, excludes them from the hierarchical order of the Church, they can not be divorced from the life and purity of the Church, for monastic life evolves from the life of the Church itself, even from the counsels The Gospel is based on God's word and example. The writer will explain this in chapters two and four of this project paper.

http://bruderfic.or.id/h-37/, **Tuesday 26 September 2017**

This article was written by one brother of FIC Congregation and as a whole, it is written in the Indonesian Language. The author of the article explains the understanding of what a brother is and what the brothers do, like teaching. If someone becomes a brother not seek honours. It is also necessary to have confidence that a brother is called to be a brother, not to be another. Then the writer uses this article in chapter three of this project paper talks about The Figure of Brother in the Mind of Indonesian People.

> "*The FIC Brothers are a worldwide religious community within the Catholic church whose mission is the evangelization of the poor through the provision of Christian education, formation and teaching, of the most neglected youth. We commit ourselves to following Jesus Christ by living simple lives in community, praying together and by living the three vows of poverty, celibacy and obedience. FIC stand for "the Brothers of the Immaculate Conception of the Blessed Virgin Mary". The congregation was founded in 1840 by Fr. Louis Rutten in The Netherlands.*"

CHAPTER THREE

Objective and Significance

There is a proverb or saying that if one does not know then one cannot love. One needs to know a person, before being in love with that person. So, "to know" is the first step to take before loving. So it is the case in the Brother's vocation. The writer, himself sometimes thinks and asks why many people still keep out of mind or out of their thinking about Brothers' vocation. The first reason that appears in my mind is that they do not know well who the Brothers are.

On the other hand, we can find only a few people, young people, enter the religious congregation and become a Brother. Most people choose to become priests. The writer does not think that this is a problem or struggle in Brother's vocation. In fact, there is an unknown about Brother's vocation.

To help young people and candidates in initial formation to know, love and eventually choose to be religious brothers, the writer assumes the main pastoral objective of the project as an attempt to design a **"come and see" program. It is a three-day formation program to appreciate the vocation of the Salesian Brother in India."**

In order to respond adequately to the main pastoral objective of this project, it will be necessary to answer the following questions:

1. What is the religious Brother's vocation in the Church?
2. What is the vocation of the Salesian Brother?

3. What is the role of the Salesian Brother in the Salesian Congregation?

4. How can this formation program assist young people as the Salesian's candidate in initial formation to grow in knowledge and then continue their human, intellectual, spiritual and pastoral formation?

5. What recommendations can be drawn from this project?

This book hopes to be meaningful for the following reasons:

For youth ministry – There have been many project papers written about how to do Pastoral Youth Ministry for young people. However, there appears to be lacking any formation program to train those who have applied for the religious brotherhood to be seen as youth pastoral ministers. This project paper is a response to this need and at the same time responding to the call of the Church, to have a special "program of brotherly training" which is to be undertaken by each formation house.

For Indian Delegation (in preparation to be a Vice-Province) – This study will certainly help the delegate and his council in the Indian Delegation as well as the director of the candidate to rediscover the great task of formation of new candidates. In India, we have many vocations to become religious men and women. But to be religious brothers, only a few young people decide to join. This formation program might help the young people especially those young people in the initial formation to know, understand, and finally decide to become a brother knowing about this vocation.

For the young candidate in initial formation – This book might help the young candidate in initial formation. They can use it to study, to know and to love the Salesian Brother vocation. Then, in the end, some of them may find or discover their vocation and decide to become a Salesian Brother. So the writer attempts this project paper to help them come to a decision freely and knowingly.

For the writer – This book helps the writer to answer the question of where the values of brotherhood life come from. This question has always triggered his mind since the day of his first profession. The fundamental values are rooted in the biblical teaching and the life of Jesus. The understanding of these values has been in the religious life experience of the Salesian Brothers. This milieu of Salesian Brotherhood among the confreres and the meaningful camaraderie of the Indian Salesian Brothers have been especially potent to appreciate the Salesian Brother's vocation.

CHAPTER FOUR

The Vocation TO BROTHERHOOD

Speaking about vocation, we believe that all men and women have their personal call to mission. There are many kinds of vocations, like marriage (parents), religious women and men, and priests. In this chapter, the writer would focus on the Salesian brotherhood vocation. This chapter is divided into three sections: Brotherhood as a Vocation in the Church, the Vocation of the Salesian Brother and The Role of the Salesian Brother in the Salesian Congregation.

A. BROTHERHOOD AS A VOCATION IN THE CHURCH

As we have presented briefly in Chapter I, there are sufficient sources or official Church documents explaining the place and identity of the consecrated lifestyle of Brothers called in the Church. The Second Vatican Council, in the document *Perfectae Caritatis* art. 10, states that "Religious life of lay members, for men and women, is a status of practising the complete Gospel Counsels. Thus, the Sacred Council greatly appreciates religious life, as meritorious to continue the pastoral duties of the Church, like as the education of the youth, the care of the sick, and other ministries. The Council affirms its these religious in their vocation, and encourages them to adapt their lives to the demands of the present times."[1] Pope John Paul II in *Vita Consecrata* art.1 says, at all times there are men and women who obey the Father's call and the encouragement of the Holy Spirit and choose that particular way of following Christ to dedicate themselves with an undivided heart. Like the

Apostles, they too have left everything to be one with Christ and as He devotes himself to God and to their brothers and sisters. Thus, through the many charisms of the Spiritual and Apostolic life, given to them by the Holy Spirit, they help make the mystery and mission of the Church radiant and thus participate in the renewal of society. And then in art. 60 it says, that according to the traditional doctrine of the Church, the Consecrated Life by its nature is neither lay nor clerical.

Recently (2015), the Congregation for Institutes of Consecrated Life and Societies of Apostolic Life the religious life issued a document entitled "Identity and Mission of the Religious Brother in the Church. Through this document, the Church once again affirms the importance and significance of the religious brothers in the Church. The document calls the religious brother a living memorial for the Church's awareness of her identity and mission as People of God.

In the book, *Iman Katolik*, KWI (Indonesian bishops' conference) it is written, "Brothers and Sisters are not members of the hierarchy, and all nuns do not belong to the hierarchy. There may be monks who are ordained priests. They are at the same time members of the monastic order, and an auxiliary group of the bishop, but living in a monastic way is not an ecclesiastical function, but a feature of life.[2]

Perhaps some of these quotations can be clarified by an understanding of what is the brother's vocation in the Church. That the vocation of the brother is a development of the consecration conferred by the Sacraments of Baptism and of the faith, through which he fully lives the Christian values of the People of God: sanctified and sent by God the Father for the salvation of the world, and participates in the mission and action of Christ a prophet, priest, and shepherd, and so fits in the Church's own mission to witness and proclaim the Gospel.

B. THE VOCATION OF THE SALESIAN BROTHER

When the writer entered the Salesian community, he witnessed two kinds of Salesian vocation, priests and brothers, that support each other. At that time, there were three brothers present among us in our community. Priests or brothers were happy and did many things together, except when the priest was the only one to offer Mass. The brothers dedicated their time in the workshop (training centre) to educating the young people and students. The writer found out that Salesian Brother's vocation was in demand.

As the General Chapter 21 (GC21) says that the Salesian Coadjutor (now is Salesian Brother – SB) is not an "ecclesiastic" and not merely a "layman" but SB is a baptized person called by God to give himself totally to Him in Christ, to serve him as a "lay religious" in the Salesian Congregation for young people. In it and in communion with the Salesian priest, Don Bosco creates the specific mission of promoting the integral Christian education of young people, especially the poorest.[3]

In the Constitutions of the Salesians,[4] article 22 says that each one of us is called by God to form part of the Salesian Society. Because of this God gives him personal gifts, and faithful correspondence so that he finds his way to complete fulfilment in Christ. And in article 96 it says, that He (God) calls us to live out in the Church our Founder's project as apostles of the young. We respond to this call by committing ourselves to an adequate ongoing formation, for which the Lord daily gives us his grace.

From these sources above (GC21 and Constitution of the Salesians of Francis de Sales) we can know that all vocations in the Salesian Society, priests or brothers, are from God. God is the initiator calling those people who will continue his mission for these times and needs. So the origin of the Brother's religious call is a profound experience of God's love. "We experience the love of God, and therefore we believe" (cf. 1 Joh 4:16).

In Acts of the General Council, it says that as religious, we Salesians are called to the radical approach of the gospel in consecrated life. In our reflection, in our way of living and acting in practice with reference to God's call. A vocation is not chosen but given; we can only recognize it and welcome it; so too with the radical approach of the gospel, before being a commitment and a task is a gift and grace. Therefore, a vocation does not come from one's personal initiative, since it is a call to a specific mission, which is not determined by us but by the One who calls. There is a Person who gazes at you, loves you and calls you and you can accept or refuse the proposal. To a personal appeal, one can reply "yes" or "no". All this happens with the greatest freedom.[5]

Great freedom, therefore, is required to give of oneself totally and hand oneself over to the Person Beloved. Obviously, in order to leave everything and to give oneself totally to Someone, one needs to be very much in love. The book "The Salesian Brother," says self-sacrificing dedication to others leads to the development of the vocation itself.[6]

The writer, personally, thinks if a person becomes a Brother, this is a call and a choice. An option or choice that cannot be influenced nor forced by anyone. The aspect of freedom is very important. In retrospect, one chooses to be "a Brother" because he has seen examples of witnessing the way of life and the work of predecessor brothers, either through direct experience of living with these or through models seen in the biographical books of the brothers. These inspirational examples influence the brother to step on the option with joy.

The other reason and more reflective is the calling of a brother who is kept alive by the encouragement of the Holy Spirit to follow God's will and surrender in the three religious professions: to be obedient, poor and pure.

C. THE ROLE OF THE SALESIAN BROTHER IN THE SALESIAN CONGREGATION

The presence of the Salesian Brother (SB) in the Salesians of Don Bosco Congregation is very special. This is evident in SB as a religious with the lay element. The SB is an element that enriches the mission of the Congregation. In the book "The Project of Life" the author explains the role of the Salesian Brothers:[7]

1. The Rule presents the Salesian Brother, in the first place, in his singular Salesian vocation, as a "brilliant creation of the great heart of Don Bosco, inspired by Mary Help of Christians." The choice to be a brother(s) has opted for a positive Christian ideal, constituted by a number of values which form of themselves and have become the time vocational choice high quality.

2. As a Salesian, the Brother is first and foremost an *"educator,"* dedicated by vow to the overall advancement of the young and the common people. He carries out tasks of a cultural, professional, social and financial kind, in addition to those which are of a catechetical, liturgical and missionary in nature; in other words, he is engaged in *"every field of education and pastoral activity"*. Because, as a religious, he does not act in his own name but receives his mission from the Church, he shares deeply in the pastoral ministry, giving a particular expression to his baptismal priesthood.

3. The brother also gives his characteristic contribution to the community, a contribution which the Constitutions see as deriving precisely from his lay condition. As Don Bosco said, "there are some things that priests and clerics cannot do, and you (Salesian Brother) able to do them"[8]. Those things are precisely the things which condition him as a "lay" religious enables the Salesian Brother to do.

4. The traditional name of "Salesian Brother" is the term "Lay Salesian" in the Constitutions and Regulations. The 'lay' form in which the brother lives, explains clearly in the GC21 that the lay dimension is the concrete form in which the brother lives and operates as a Salesian Religious. So this is his specific characteristic, a significant and essential value of his identity.

5. The 'specific qualities of his lay status,' distinguish him from the other the lay qualities of the man living in the world. As the brother with the characteristics proper to religious life, he lives his vocation as a member of the laity, seeking the Kingdom of God by engaging in temporal affairs and by ordering them according to God's plan; he exercises his baptismal priesthood, prophetic witness and kingly service, and in this way truly shares in the life and mission of Christ in the Church (spreading the Gospel and sanctifying in a non-sacramental manner); his works of charity are undertaken with greater dedication within a Congregation devoted to the integral education of youth, especially those in need; finally, as regards the Christian renewal in the temporal order, since he has renounced worldliness he exercises this form of apostolate as a religious in a most efficacious manner, educating youth to the Christian renewal of work and to other human values.

6. The reality of his lay status is not cancelled by his religious profession, but rather gives a special slant to every aspect of the confrere's life: the Salesian mission, the life of a community, apostolic activity, a profession of the counsels, prayer and the spiritual life. As Don Bosco wanted: enriched by its lay aspect the community is able to approach the world more validly as regards its apostolic objectives.

7. His lay condition and his experience, united with a deeply Salesian heart, make him particularly "close ... to the young and to the realities of working life". His Salesian heart is anchored in the transcendence he lives in temporal realities into which he injects the radical power of the Gospel. This enables him to move in a secular context with a mentality which is at the same time both "technical" and "pastoral," and this is of great value to the community.

The writer can say that the choice to be a priest or brother is actually the same, that is, "the Salesian calling." The book "Project of Life" says that they are presented in the first place in their fundamental equality. The Salesian vocation is the same for both and each is a "Salesian."[9] Both are the complementary faces of Don Bosco, in task and work.

And in his experience, the duties and ministry of the brothers are real presences in the midst of such people as in dormitories, workshops and schools.

To the Don Bosco Salesian Coadjutor (Salesian Brother) is pointed out as a specific path to holiness in the provision of various services to the Community: Administrative and Managerial Responsibilities of particular sectors; Educational and Apostolic tasks; Missionary Evangelizing activities and a wide range of other activities. He shows the necessity and richness of their presence in the Congregation as participants in the apostolic work of the community in carrying out duties best suited to the layperson and the priest and in the possibility of bringing a Christian witness and their evangelizing work wherever it would be for the priest unsuitable or impossible to arrive.[10]

In our Holy Book, the Constitution of the Salesians of Francis de Sales are some articles about us as Salesians and especially the Brothers:[11]

a. Article 6 says that the Salesian vocation places us at the heart of the Church and puts us entirely at the service of her mission.

b. Article 14 says that our vocation is graced by a special gift of God: a predilection for the young.

c. Article 15 says that we are sent to the young people by the God who is 'all charity', the Salesian is open and cordial, ready to make the first approach and to welcome others with unfailing kindliness, respect and patience.

d. And article 45 says that the Salesian Brother brings to every field of education and pastoral activity the specific qualities of his lay status, which make him in a particular way of being witness to God's Kingdom in the world, close as he is to the young and to the realities of working life. The significant and complementary presence of clerical and lay Salesians in the community constitutes an essential element of its make-up and of its apostolic completeness.

In the book of the Ratio, there is mention that the Salesian Brother "combines in himself the gifts of consecration with those of the lay state": he lives in the lay state as a consecrated person. "The presence of the Salesian Brother enriches the apostolic activity of the community. It reminds the priest members of the values inherent in the lay religious vocation and recalls to them constantly an active collaboration with laypeople. It also recalls to the Salesian priests the vision of an apostolic goal and ideal that is complex in its reality, because it goes beyond priestly and catechetical activity in the strict sense." He has a significant role to play, especially in certain contexts where the priest is seen as a sacred or cultic figure. By his consecrated life the Salesian Brother proclaims the presence of God in daily life, the importance of becoming disciples before being teachers, and bears witness to a convinced life of faith not tied to functional or ministerial duties.[12]

The writer understands that the Salesian Brother's contribution to mission and community is the same, of the Salesian Priest who dedicates his life to the young people who are in need. On the other hand, his mission is following the specialization for which he has prepared. So, he shares his knowledge, ability, and skill with the young people of the community to which he is sent.

[1] Vatican Council II, *Perfectae Caritatis*, Austin Flannery, O.P. (General Editor), New Revised Edition (Pasay City - Philippines: Paulines Publishing House, 2007), 616.

[2] Konferensi Waligereja Indonesia, *Iman Katolik: Buku Informasi dan Referensi* (Indonesia: Kanisius and Obor, 1996), 375.

[3]http://www.sdb.org/en/salesiani-di-don-bosco/capitoli-generali/498-cg21-1978/1280-cg-21- documento-2-1978. Taken 20 November 2017.

[4]*Constitutions of The Society of St Francis de Sales*, Third edition (India, 2009), 30 and 85.

[5]*Acts of the General Council of the Salesian Society of Don Bosco*, year XCIII, N. 413 (Rome, 8 April 2012), 22-23.

[6]*The Salesian Brother: History, Identity Vocational Apostolate and Formation* (Rome 1989 and published by Don Bosco Makati Press, Philippines), 73.

[7] Fr. George Williams SDB (translator), *The Project of Life of The Salesians of Don Bosco: A Guide to the Salesian Constitutions* (Madras – India, 1987), 416

[8]*The Salesian Brother*, 27.

[9]*Project of Life*, 414.

[10]http://www.sdb.org/en/salesiani-di-don-bosco/capitoli-generali/498-cg21-1978/1280-cg-21- documento-2-1978. Taken by 20 November 2017. In Don Bosco's time the name of Salesian Brother is Salesian Coadjutor (SC).

[11]*Constitutions*, 20, 25 and 49.

[12]*Formation of Salesians of Don Bosco: Principles and Norms, Ratio Fundamentalis Institutionis et Studiorum*, Third Edition (Rome, 2009), 49-50.

CHAPTER FIVE

Toward an appreciation for the Salesian Brothers' Vocation

In this chapter, the writer will present "A Three-day Formation Program for postulants / pre-novices." The process that the writer used in producing the project will be briefly explained and followed by the program itself and the process results.

General Considerations

There were several congregations of brothers who have long worked in India. But most people do not know and understand exactly the call of a brother. One reason is that people are more familiar with the figure of a priest. This is supported by the evolving situation and conditions of calling which most of the priestly figures are visible in pastoral work.

This prompted the author to make a three-day coaching program for postulants / pre-novices. The author considers that there are candidates who have not to understand the call of a Salesian brother. They can be called "tabula rasa" about the call to brotherhood.

There are three things to talk about: *God calls and Man responds, The Challenges and Difficulties* and *the Beauty of the Salesian Brother Vocation*. Through these three days of coaching programs, they can know, and love and they choose freely to become Salesian Brothers.

Presented below are the general objectives of the catechetical program or retreat for Aspirantate/postulants:

1. To make them understand and appreciate God's call

2. To make them understand the vocation of Salesian Brother

3. Through deep reflection, they can decide to choose to be Salesian Brother

4. To make them understand the place and role of Salesian Brother in Salesian Congregation
5. To make them understand and remain faithful to the challenge and the joy of the Salesian Brothers.

Here are some resources:

1. **Suggested venue**: possibly, a retreat centre (with room accommodation, the main session hall, a dining hall) or any venue where there is access to a chapel or catholic church and a priest to celebrate the Holy Eucharist, hear confession, preside an exposition of the Blessed Sacrament as suggested by the program.
2. **Suggested speaker**: Salesian Brother or Priest preferably with experience in this program.
3. **Material needed**: specific materials needed for each session will be detailed in the module outline, but generally, the main session needs to have a laptop, a projector, a band set-up and a good sound system for the duration of the whole program.
4. **Service team**: for the duration of the retreat, depending on the member of participants, the following people should compose the service team – Team Leader, music ministry, discussion group leader, logistics, secretariat and program committees to make sure that the program runs smoothly and all the required materials are provided for.

Here are two things that the writer would present: the program schedule and modules of the Catechetical program.

Program Schedule

In the matrix below is a suggested schedule on how the entire program can be run in a three-day set-up, which the writer highly proposes. The spiritual and pastoral experience of the participants can best be maximized in this kind of setup. However, if the schedule won't permit a weekend seminar retreat, the catechetical program can still be implemented in a series type where one module can be given per week. If this is the case, the program will be finished after 5 weekends (one module per week).

Modules of the Catechetical Program

The table below presents the syllabus of the whole program. Following this will be the detailed outlines of the modules containing all the session dynamics.

Day	Theme of the day	Objectives	Biblical, Constitution foundation and story
1	**God calls and Man responds**	a. To hear, to understand and aware the Gods Call b. Reflect and discernment their vocation c. To respond and follow God's call in daily life. d. Say "YES" to God's call every day.	*Biblical*: Mark 1:16-20; 2:14-15; 3:13-19. *Constitution*: articles 22 and 94 *Story*: John's dream at the age of nine (1825).
2	**The Challenges and Difficulties to the vocation**	1. To know the source of challenges and difficulties 2. To make personal solution or trick in facing the challenges and difficulties.	
3	**The Beauty of the Salesian Brother Vocation**	1. To know that is God's calling 2. To understand and accept the free choice and decision 3. To know the role of the SB in Congregation 4. Live in vows and community	

CHAPTER SIX

Day 1 – God calls and Man responds (Module 1)

Rationale: Speaking about vocation, we believe that all men and women have their personal call to mission. There are many kinds of vocations, like marriage (parents), religious women and men, and priests. God is the initiator to call anyone to do His mission. So, the one who is called has a right and freedom to answer it. We too freely answer God's call to this religious life.

Objectives. At the end of this session, the aspirants/postulants are expected to:

1. Have the courage to answer God's call.
2. To hear, understand and be aware the God's Call
3. Reflect and discern their vocation
4. To respond to and follow God's call in daily life.
5. Say "YES" to God's call every day.

Introduction: (Input Session 1)
Vocations, the Gift of the Love of God.[1]
"What I am is God's gift to me. What I become is my gift to God."
These words bring to mind how we are called in unique ways to live our lives, to serve Christ and one another, whether it is as a single person, a married couple, a consecrated person or as an ordained person. Discovering our vocation is both exciting and challenging. To help us discover our vocation, Pope Benedict XVI,

on the 49th World Day of Prayer for Vocations, invites us to reflect on the theme: "Vocations, the Gift of the love of God." The 49th World Day of Prayer for Vocations is an opportunity for us to focus in particular on the vocations of consecrated life and the ordained ministry. The 49th World Day of Prayer for Vocations will be celebrated on 29th April 2012.

Vocation is a gift from God who calls all of us to create and foster relationships that will enable us to partake in the mission of the Church. In his message, Pope Benedict reminds us that "the source of every perfect gift is God who is Love." We are invited to respond freely to this gift that God himself has given us. Our response to this must be generous, free and open as we try to discern the will of God in our lives. Vocation is more than a call; it is also a mission to let others be aware of it as well. It is a mission that invites us to come, to follow Christ and be "fishers of men."

Vocation and Hindrances

The word vocation comes from *vocare*, a Latin verb that means "to call." When we talk about a call, it is implied that there is an existence of a caller (someone who calls) and a

respondent (someone who receives the call). God is the caller, as someone who wants to speak and communicate with us. We are therefore recipients of the call, and as such, we are invited to listen and heed the message.

Unfortunately, we fail to recognize, and thus fail to answer this call. The emergence of consumerism and secularism somehow gives a distorted view of 'being' and 'having'. It is often asserted that to be or to have is based on one's wealth, success and power. This becomes the measure of one's dignity and rights. Such preoccupations in life may become a hindrance to our listening to God's call. We must cultivate an interior silence and peace of mind for us to listen and heed the call of God, our very own vocation.

Vocation in Scriptures

There are many vocation stories in the scriptures: Abraham, Moses, Jeremiah, Isaiah, the twelve apostles and Paul were just some of the vocation stories. They listened and generously responded to the Lord's call, which transformed their lives into a mission of following the Lord and sharing the Good News with all people.

Each of us has his/her own story of a vocation. Every individual is called, no matter whatever and wherever he/she is. Vocations most of the time begin from personal experiences that move the person to follow and commit oneself to such a call.

Pastores Dabo Vobis

In his apostolic exhortation, I Will Give You Shepherds - *Pastores Dabo Vobis*, Blessed John Paul II explains that each vocation comes from God and is God's gift (PDV #35). Vocation is rooted in one's life experiences. It is an invitation for every person to accept and listen to God's call. On our part, it is a free response to God, a sign of commitment and dedication to love and service.

Similarly, Pope Benedict, in his message on the 49th World Day of Prayer for Vocations, reminds us that "Every human person is the fruit of God's thought and an act of his love, a love that is boundless, faithful and everlasting. It is a love that is limitless and that precedes us, sustains us and calls us along the path of life, a love rooted in an absolutely free gift of God... Every specific vocation is born of the initiative of God; it is a gift of the Love of God!"

Be Open to God's Love

We need to open our lives to this love. It is to the perfection of the Father's love (cf. Mt 5:48) that Jesus Christ calls us every day! The high standard of the Christian life consists in loving 'as' God loves; with a love that is shown in the total, faithful and fruitful gift of self. Saint John of the Cross, writing to the Prioress of the Monastery of Segovia who was pained by the terrible circumstances surrounding his suspension, responded by urging her to act as God does: 'Think nothing else but that God ordains all, and where there is no love, put love, and there you will draw out love' (Letters, 26).

It is in this soil of self-offering and openness to the love of God, and as the fruit of that love, that all vocations are born and grow. By drawing from this wellspring through prayer, constant recourse to God's word and the sacraments, especially the Eucharist, it becomes possible to live a life of love for our neighbours, in whom we come to perceive the face of Christ the Lord (see Mt 25:31-46). To express the inseparable bond that links these 'two loves' ... love of God and love of neighbour... both of which flow from the same divine source and return to it, Pope Saint Gregory the Great uses the metaphor of the seedling: 'In the soil of our heart God first planted the root of love for him; from this, like the leaf, sprouts love for one another.'

Priesthood and Religious Life (Brotherhood) are Lives of Deep Joy

These two expressions of the one divine love must be lived with a particular intensity and purity of heart by those who have decided to set out on the path of vocation discernment towards the ministerial priesthood and the consecrated life; they are its distinguishing mark. Love of God, which priests and consecrated persons are called to mirror, however imperfectly, is the motivation for answering the Lord's call to special consecration through priestly ordination or the profession of the evangelical counsels. Saint Peter's vehement reply to the Divine Master: 'Yes, Lord, you know that I love you (John 21:15) contains the secret of a life fully given and lived out, and thus deeply joyful one.

The other practical expression of love, that towards our neighbour, and especially those who suffer and are in greatest need, is the decisive impulse that leads the priest and the consecrated person to be a builder of communion between people and a sower of hope. The relationship of consecrated persons, and especially of the priest, to the Christian community is vital and becomes a fundamental dimension of their affectivity.

The task of fostering vocations will be to provide helpful guidance and direction along the way. Central to this should be the love of God's word nourished by a growing familiarity with *Sacred Scripture*, and attentive and unceasing *prayer*, both personal and in the community; this will make it possible to hear God's call amid all the voices of daily life. But above all, *the Eucharist* should be the heart of every vocational journey: it is here that the love of God touches us in Christ's sacrifice, the perfect expression of love, and it is here that we learn ever anew how to live according to the 'high standard' of God's love. *Scripture, prayer* and *the Eucharist* are the precious treasure enabling us to grasp the beauty of a life spent fully in service of the Kingdom.

Conclusion:

Vocation is a gift from God who calls all of us to create and foster relationships that will enable us to partake in the mission of the Church. In his message, Pope Benedict reminds us that "the source of every perfect gift is God who is Love." We are invited to respond freely to this gift that God himself has given us. Our response to this must be generous, free and open as we try to discern the will of God in our lives. Vocation is more than a call; it is also a mission to let others be aware of it as well. It is a mission that invites us to come, follow Christ and be "fishers of men."

Vocation is a gift of God's grace which encourages every person to fill one's heart and mind with gratitude, trust and hope in the Lord who summons every person to holiness and service to others.

Closing activity:

Before the session closes formally, the participants will be divided into groups sharing which will also serve as their cell group for the entire weekend. They will be asked to reflect and share their awareness on the following question:

1). Can I remember the first reasons why I chose my vocation?

2). How did I discover the deepest aspects?

3. What is my reason today?

4. From the vocation story in the Scripture, to whom do you attract?

The session speaker will conclude the talk and end it with a vocation prayer

Vocation Prayer

Lord of all goodness, all is a gift from you. May I trust you with all my heart? You love and accept me unconditionally and desire only what is best for me. Guide me to know that desire and help me to fulfil my vocation in life. Help me to know with conviction that path in life you call me to so that I may say YES freely, joyfully and follow you wherever you lead me. Amen.

Introduction: (Input Session 2)

Some questions are often asked by people when they meet a religious Brother: "What is a Religious Brother?" "What do they do?" "Why be a religious brother?" "Why just be a religious brother and not go to be a priest?" "Why not be a priest?" "Can a brother become a priest?" and so many other questions!

We sometimes encounter the wrong conclusions about the vocation of a Salesian Brother. Someone would conclude that since a Salesian Brother does not continue in studies like his clerical confreres, he doesn't need to be excelling in his trade and education – this is not the case – The Salesian Brother pursues his calling by making himself an educator for the young, in their settings.

But if traced further to the meaning of a call, it is quite different. The difference cannot be properly understood by people in general. Why? In sum, the call to brotherhood is very rare whereas the call to priesthood is more common, although lately there has been a decline in vocations to the priesthood.

Some Thoughts from the documents

Sufficient sources or official Church documents are explaining the position and identity of the consecrated lifestyle of brothers called in the Church. For example, The Second Vatican Council, in the document *Perfectae Caritatis* art. 10, states that the Religious life of lay members, for men and women, is a status of practising the complete gospel counsels. Thus, the Sacred Council greatly appreciates it, as so meritorious to the pastoral duties of the Church, through the education of the youth, the care of the sick, and the other ministries. The Council affirms its members in their vocation and encourages them to adapt their lives to the demands of the present times.[2] In addition we can also find in *Lumen Gentium* art. 43, that "This status of life has its place in the structure of the ecclesiastical hierarchy. The status of this vocation is not a middle way between the vocation of the priest and the laity. This call should be regarded as a special vocation for Christians, enabling them to enjoy special grace within the Church, and in each way contributing to the Church's rescue mission."[3] *Vita Consecrata* art.1 says, every time some men and women obey the Father's call and the encouragement of the Holy Spirit and choose that particular way of following Christ to dedicate himself to his undivided heart. Like the Apostles, they too have left everything to be one with Christ and as He devotes himself to God and their brothers and sisters. Thus, through the many charisms of the spiritual and apostolic life, given to them by the Holy Spirit, they help make the mystery and mission of the Church radiant and thus participate in the renewal of society. And then in art. 60 says, that according to the traditional doctrine of the Church, the consecrated life by its nature is neither lay nor clerical. This statement has existed in *The Code of Canon Law*, canon 588 §1. For this reason, the "lay consecration" of both men and women constitutes a state which in its profession of the evangelical counsels is complete in itself. Consequently, both for the individual and the Church, it has a value in itself, apart from the sacred ministry.[4] In the book *Iman Katolik*, KWI (Indonesian bishops' conference) is written, Brothers and Sisters are not members of the hierarchy, and all the nuns do not belong to the hierarchy. It's just that there are monks who are ordained priests. They are at the same time members of the monastic and auxiliary group of the bishop, but living in a monastic way is not an ecclesiastical function, but a feature of life. Therefore, the Second Vatican Council teaches, even though the status embodied by the exposition of gospel counsels, excludes them from the hierarchical order of the Church, but also cannot be divorced from the life and purity of the Church, for monastic life evolves from the life of the Church itself, even counsel The Gospel is based on God's word and example.[5]

Then our congregation teaches that the Salesian Brother "combines in himself the gifts of consecration with those of the lay state": he lives in the lay state as a consecrated person. "The presence of Salesian Brother enriches the apostolic activity of the community. It reminds the clerical section of the values inherent in the lay religious vocation and recalls them constantly to an active collaboration with laypeople. It also recalls to the Salesian priests the vision of an apostolic goal and ideal that is complex in its reality, because it goes beyond priestly and catechetical activity in the strict sense." The Salesian Brother has a significant role to play, especially in certain contexts where the priest is seen as a sacred or cultic figure. By his consecrated life he proclaims the presence of God in daily life, and the importance of becoming disciples before being teachers, and bears witness to a convinced life of faith not tied to functional or ministerial duties.[6]

The writer, personally, thinks if a person becomes a brother, this is a call and a choice. An option or choice that cannot be influenced forced by anyone. The aspect of freedom is very important. In addition, one chooses to be a brother because he has seen examples of witness from the way of life and the work of predecessor brothers, either through direct experience of living with these or through models seen in the biographical books of the brothers. These inspirational examples influence the brother to step on the option with joy.

Some testimonies

Here are some testimonies of some brothers from different congregation:[7]

1. Br. Conrad Richardson, FBP (Franciscan Brother of Peace) said, "God calls some men to be priests, some to be brothers and some to be priest-brothers. Each vocation is distinct and complete. My life as a brother is filled with great joy and of course, there are hefty challenges as well. Let's face it, life isn't easy no matter what vocation we are called to, but I know that with God's saving

grace and with the help of my brothers, I will continue to grow in love with Him and all those around me. May God be praised, both now and forever!"

2. Brother Crispin Mary, CFR (The Community of the Franciscan Friars of the Renewal) said, "God is so good to bring me to the vocation of the lay brother. Poverty, minority, and a simple life are exactly the cross I need in order to be recreated in God's image. Now I am an apprentice at the Holy House of Nazareth in the South Bronx where the pursuit of prayer life, gestures of fraternal service, simple living—and yes, even doing things like cleaning out the drain pipes at the shelter—is the path to Heaven!"

3. Brother Patrick Reilly, BH (Brother of Hope) said, "Living now as a vowed Brother is a great gift, knowing that I'm following what God has been calling me to. It's a summons to hold nothing back from Him and to give everything to the One who gave everything for me. I consider it the greatest joy of my life."

[1] This part is taken from https://lifeteen.com/blog/vocations-the-gift-of-the-love-of-god/ and http://www.cam.org.au/vocations/Article-View/Article/14611/A-gift-that-keeps-on-giving.

[2] Austin Flannery, O.P. (General Editor), Vatican Council II, *Perfectae Caritatis*, New Revised Edition (Pasay City - Philippines: Paulines Publishing House, 2007), 616.

[3] *Ibid.*, *Lumen Gentium*, 403.

[4] John Paul II, *Vita Consacrata* (Pasay City - Philippines: Paulines Publishing House, 2015), 82.

[5] Konferensi Waligereja Indonesia, *Iman Katolik* (Indonesia: Kanisius and Obor, 1996), 375.

[6] Formation of Salesians of Don Bosco: Principles and Norms, Ratio Fundamentalis Institutionis et Studiorum, Third Editionn (Rome, 2009), 49-50.

[7] It is taken from http://www.religiousbrotherhood.com/testimonies/.

CHAPTER SEVEN

Day 2 – The Challenges and Difficulties (Module 2)

The Salesian Brother Vocation

The writer had an experience as a brother. When he entered the Salesian community, he saw two kinds of Salesian vocation, priests and brothers, that supported each other. At that time, there were three brothers present among us in our community. Priests or brothers were happy and did many things together, except what pertains to the priest ministry. The brothers spent their time in the workshop (training centre) with the young people and students. He found that Salesian Brother's vocation was in demand.

So, in the novitiate, he wrote a letter asking to become a Salesian Brother. His Novice Master found out his choice to be a Salesian Brother, he then said, "if one day, a younger priest becomes a rector, would you obey him?" "Yes, he replied, because Don Bosco said we should obey our rector as he is." Then he was smiling at me. On another day, he approached the writer and said that he did not believe that his choice was decided as yet. Until he made my perpetual profession, he supported my vocation. Finally, he made it and he prayed that God protects and guides me until the end.

And after he became a Salesian Brother (with temporary vows) he visited his family for the first time. They asked him about my vocation. Would he someday be a priest? And he replied that he is a brother and will be a Brother. Some of his brothers did not understand it. In his place, when one enters the seminary, it means he will become a priest. But he explained to them that in a Salesian family we are the same, either brother or priest. His aunt said, "It is ok, as long as he is happy, and enjoys his vocation!" On hearing his aunt's comment, he felt it was like God's voice and he was happy to hear it. The General Chapter 21 (GC21) says that the Salesian Coadjutor (now is Salesian Brother – SB) is not an "ecclesiastic" and not merely a "layman" but SB is a baptized person called by God to give himself totally to Him in Christ, to serve him as a "lay religious" in the Salesian Congregation for young people.

The Constitutions of the Salesians,[8] article 22 says that each one of us is called by God to form part of the Salesian Society. Because of this God gives him personal gifts, and faithful correspondence so that he finds his way to complete fulfilment in Christ. And in article 96 it says, that He (God) calls us to live out in the Church our Founder's project as apostles of the young. We respond to this call by committing ourselves to an adequate ongoing formation, for which the Lord daily gives us his grace.

The Acts of the General Council says that as religious, we Salesians are called to the radical approach of the gospel in consecrated life. In our reflection, in our way of living and acting in practice with reference to God's call. A vocation is not chosen but given; we can only recognize it and welcome it. So too with the radical approach to the gospel. Before being a commitment and a task is a gift and grace. Therefore, a vocation does not come from one's personal initiative, since it is a call to a specific mission, which is not determined by us but by the One who calls. There is a Person who gazes at you, loves you and calls you and you can accept or refuse the proposal. To a personal appeal, one can reply "yes" or "no." All this happens with the greatest freedom.[9]

Great freedom, therefore, is required to give of oneself totally and hand oneself over to the Person Beloved. Obviously, in order to leave everything and to give oneself totally to Someone, one needs to be very much in love. The book "The Salesian Brother," says self-sacrificing dedication to others leads to the development of the vocation itself.[10]

The writer, personally, thinks if a person becomes a Brother, this is a call and a choice. An option or choice that cannot be influenced nor forced by anyone. The aspect of freedom is very important. In retrospect, one chooses to be "a Brother" because he has seen examples of witnessing the way of life and the work of predecessor brothers, either through direct experience of living with these or through models seen in the biographical books of the brothers. These inspirational examples influence the brother to step on the option with joy.

The other reason, more reflective, is the calling of a brother kept alive by the encouragement of the Holy Spirit to follow God's will and surrender to the three religious professions: to be obedient, poor and pure.

Challenges and Difficulties

Here are some challenges and difficulties that make the brother humble in their vocation and more courageous to show the people that the vocation as brother is grace and loving.

In Common

The misunderstood about the brotherhood vocation. First, from the parents and family who could not understand why their son was not for the priesthood. He says this because he himself had experienced it. And many people have a wish that if one enters seminary or religious life, in the end, he becomes a priest. Not a brother. Second, among priests and members of the hierarchy, there is a general lack of understanding or even awareness of the vocation of a Religious Brother. It is not uncommon to hear bishops address their "brother- priests" and the "religious sisters" when speaking before an assembly and miss out on the Religious Brothers even on occasions when the Brothers are visibly present.[11] Third, we sometimes encounter the wrong conclusions about the vocation of a Salesian Brother. Someone would conclude that since a Salesian Brother does not continue in studies like his clerical confreres, he doesn't need to be excelling in his own trade and education – this is not the case – The Salesian Brother pursues his calling by making himself an educator for the young, in their own settings.

But if traced further to the meaning of a call, it is in fact quite different. The difference cannot be properly understood by people in general. Why? Prefer the call to brotherhood is very rare whereas the call to priesthood is more common, although lately there has been a decline in vocations to the priesthood.

In the History of Congregation: the term Coadjutor[12]

In 1867, Don Bosco used the term, Coadjutor. It means lay helpers or domestic, not religious. Maybe from this term, in the history of the Society, there was a tendency for some to regard the Brothers as lower class. Even though in his good night, 31 March 1876, Don Bosco said: "There is no distinction between members of the Congregation. Everyone is treated the same, artisans, young clerics, and priests. We consider ourselves brothers."

Then in 1877, in a new handwritten edition of the regulation for the House and the Oratory, Don Bosco used the term "coadjutor" for the first time to describe both the domestic helpers and lay-religious members of the Salesian Congregation. The coadjutors who belong to the Congregation must keep the practices of piety listed in their rule. So there is now a clear distinction between the domestic helpers and lay Salesians. But the term coadjutor was still used for both.

Again in 1883, somebody said at the third General Chapter held at Valdocco, "Coadjutors must be kept low...!" Don Bosco reacted sharply, "Not at all. Our Brother Coadjutors are like everyone else." In this chapter, Don Bosco wanted the lay members to continue to be called coadjutors as well as the lay helpers. However, the idea of calling the coadjutors "Brother" was discussed for the first time. Soon after this chapter, the term "coadjutor" was used only for the lay religious members of the society.

This name, coadjutor, was already a problem for contemporary Salesians, but Don Bosco did not want it changed in the Italian context and language.[13]

In the last twenty years, there has been fresh discussion as to whether the name "coadjutors" should be preserved or changed:

a. For some, this was the name given by the founder, Don Bosco. It carried with it values linked with our tradition and with so many wonderful figures of lay Salesians. To modify it would be to leave ourselves open to the risk of breaking with our roots and with the Salesian and cultural heritage of our society.

b. For others, the name "coadjutor" poorly reflects the significance of tradition and is entirely incomprehensible today outside our own environments. It brings to mind too an image characterized by a certain dependence, emargination and discrimination. This image can no longer be proposed to possible aspirants to the Salesian life. For this reason, a change was considered not only useful but even necessary.

In the light of these various arguments, and especially the fact that "our society is made up of clerics and laymen who complement each other as brothers in living out the same vocation", the renewed Constitutions have chosen for both groups the noun "Salesian" which denotes the one vocation, to be linked with "coadjutor" or "lay" and "presbyter" or "priest" (as adjectives), to specify the particular vocational form.

In this way was realized the desire on the one hand to be faithful to Don Bosco's wishes, and on the other hand to harmonize with present terminology and meet the rightful expectations of the confreres. But the intention was above all to emphasize the relationships of complete equality between priest and lay Salesians desired by our Founder and reiterated several times by his successors as an original aspect of our identity.

The term "coadjutor" makes a different way of looking at the Brothers. This term translated to English-speaking more understandable and change the old paradigm about the brother. That the brother no more as a servant, worker, and lower class.

Personal challenges

Father Pascual Chavez Villanueva said there is some aspect of challenges:[14] individualism, no real awareness of the identity of our vocation and affective dimension. *First*, there are some failings in the life of the Salesian: individualism in making pastoral decisions, the way in which free time is spent, the place is given to personal wellbeing at the expense of availability for the mission; but also, activism which leaves little room for the spiritual life, for regular study, for constant learning, for the practice of reflection. Confreres are not accustomed to *self-formation*, and some do not even feel the need for it. *Second*, often there is no real awareness of the identity of our vocation as consecrated Salesians so personal identification with the vocation itself is compromised. Rather than being dedicated to one's vocation, what seems to be of more interest is being at ease with oneself and with others. The affective and effective separation from the world of youth is on the increase; often they are not understood or recognized as being the sole reason for our existence. *Third*, is the affective dimension of the Salesian, which is little appreciated. Emotions, sentiments and affections are neglected if not ignored; education on interior life and forms of emotional expression is defective, through a lack of appropriate formation and of skilled formation personnel.

Fourth, there is an external factor that hinders our vocation: lack of faith education in the family. The description of the family as a small seminary, where faith planting and calling is still lacking.

Fifth, the biggest challenge facing the Salesian Brother and his greatest contribution is *"the work of evangelizing in the secular world."*15

His profession, whatever it might be, brings him close to the young and to ordinary people, and they are attracted to him because he looks like one of them.

In evangelization, what matters most is *the witness* of a person's life, as a Christian and a consecrated lay Salesian. This is what attracts young people and raises the question: why does he live this kind of life? The Salesian Brother leads young people to recognize the presence of God in the world, more by deeds than by words and shows them how to live a life of faith in the midst of secular affairs. Venerable Simon Srugi was a Salesian Brother who lived and worked among Muslims. They used to say, "To look at Simon and remember God were one and the same thing." They also used to say, "His presence was like the shadow of the presence of God."

Then there is the *ambience* the Salesian Brother manages to create in the group or in the workshop or school or playground. Today more than ever ambience *and disposition,* which is the result of values lived, is a powerful communicator of those values to all who come in contact with it. The Christian ambience, therefore, of the place where the Salesian Brother lives and works, exercises a powerful influence on all who are touched by it.

In third place, there is *dialogue or animation.* The words of a Salesian Brother have a particular efficacy when his heart is in love with Christ. He shows great respect for those with whom he speaks and he makes them open to love and search for the truth. He helps them to enter into themselves and encounter God there, to discover the religious dimension when they reflect more deeply on their experience and the human questions that arise. He willingly shares his faith experience with others, introducing them to Jesus Christ as the centre of his life. There is a whole work of listening and responding, of persuading and convincing.

Therefore, those challenges above do not make us afraid of our vocation but they encourage and make us aware of our decision to follow God's call.

❧❧❧

[8]*Constitutions of The Society of St Francis de Sales,* Third edition (India, 2009), 30 and 85.

[9]*Acts of the General Council of the Salesian Society of Don Bosco,* year XCIII, N. 413 (Rome, 8 April 2012), 22-23.

[10]*The Salesian Brother: History, Identity Vocational Apostolate and Formation* (Rome 1989 and published by Don Bosco Makati Press, Philippines), 73.

[11] Taken from http://www.dlsu.edu.ph/brothers/_pdf/my_vocational_journey.pdf.

[12] Bro Michael Harris, SDB, Don Bosco's History in Relation to the Salesian Brother, *East Oceania Salesian Brothers' Congress* (Hua

Hin, Thailand 18-23 August 2013), 10-11.

[13] The Salesian Brother: History, Identity Vocational Apostolate and Formation (Rome 1989), 83. There is a translator's note: the above paragraphs are a translation of the Italian text and therefore refer directly to the Constitutions in Italian. The English-speaking members of the GC22, which prepared the revised Italian text for definitive approval, decided that in order to avoid the lack of comprehensibility referred to above, which is still greater in English, the word "coadjutor" would be translated as "brother" in the English version of the Constitutions. For similar reasons, the expression "lay Salesian" and "priest Salesian" is used in the present translation where the two terms are used in apposition.

[14]Father Pascual Chavez Villanueva, SDB, Witnesses to the Radical Approach of the Gospel, *Acts of the General Council of the Salesian Society of Don Bosco*, year XCIII, N. 413 (Rome, 8 April 2012), 16-18. He was the 9th successor of Don Bosco.

[15] It is taken from http://dbfis.org/vocations/salesian-brothers/the-salesian-brother/

Day 3 – the Beauty of the Salesian Brother Vocation(Module 3)

The Place of the Salesian Brother in the Congregation

The presence of the Salesian Brother (SB) in the Salesians of Don Bosco Congregation is very special. This is evident in SB as a religious with the lay element. The SB is an element that enriches the mission of the Congregation.

In the book "The Project of Life" the author explains the role of the Salesian Brothers:[16]

1. The Rule presents the Salesian Brother, in the first place, in his singular Salesian vocation, as a "brilliant creation of the great heart of Don Bosco, inspired by Mary Help of Christians." The choice to be a brother(s) has opted for a positive Christian ideal, constituted by several values which form of themselves and have become the time vocational choice high quality.

2. As a Salesian, the Brother is first and foremost an *"educator,"* dedicated by vow to the overall advancement of the young and the common people. He carries out tasks of a cultural, professional, social and financial kind, in addition to those which are of a catechetical, liturgical and missionary in nature; in other words, he is engaged in *"every field of education and pastoral activity."* Because, as a religious, he does not act in his name but

receives his mission from the Church, he shares deeply in the pastoral ministry, giving a particular expression to his baptismal priesthood.

3. The brother also gives his characteristic contribution to the community, a contribution which the Constitutions see as deriving precisely from his lay condition.

As Don Bosco said, "there are some things that priests and clerics cannot do, and you (Salesian Brother) are able to do them."[17] Those things are precisely the things which condition him as a "lay" religious enable the Salesian Brother to do.

1. The traditional name of "Salesian Brother" is the term "Lay Salesian" in the Constitutions and Regulations. The 'lay' form in which the brother lives, explains clearly in the GC21 that the lay dimension is the concrete form in which the brother lives and operates as a Salesian Religious. So, this is his specific characteristic, a significant and essential value of his identity.

2. The 'specific qualities of his lay status', distinguish him from the other the lay qualities of the man living in the world. As the brother with the characteristics proper to religious life, he lives his vocation as a member of the laity, seeking the Kingdom of God by engaging in temporal affairs and by ordering them according to God's plan; he exercises his baptismal priesthood, prophetic witness and kingly service, and in this way truly shares in the life and mission of Christ in the Church (spreading the Gospel and sanctifying in a non-sacramental manner); his works of charity are undertaken with greater dedication within a Congregation devoted to the integral education of youth, especially those in need; finally, as regards the Christian renewal in the temporal order, since he has renounced worldliness he exercises this form of apostolate as a religious in a most efficacious manner, educating youth to the Christian renewal of work and other human values.

3. The reality of his lay status is not cancelled by his religious profession, but rather gives a special slant to every aspect of the confrere's life: the Salesian mission, a life of the community, apostolic activity, the profession of the counsels, prayer and the spiritual life. As Don Bosco wanted: enriched by its lay aspect the community can approach the world more validly as regards its apostolic objectives.

4. His lay condition and his experience, united with a deeply Salesian heart, make him particularly "close ... to the young and to the realities of working life." His Salesian heart is anchored in the transcendence he lives in temporal realities into which he injects the radical power of the Gospel. This enables him to move in a secular context with a mentality which is at the same time both "technical" and "pastoral," and this is of great value to the community.

The writer can say that the choice to be a priest or brother is actually the same, that is, "the Salesian calling." The book "Project of Life" says that they are presented in the first place in their fundamental equality. The Salesian vocation is the same for both and each is a "Salesian."[18] Both are the complementary faces of Don Bosco, in task and work. And in his experience, the duties and ministry of the brothers are real presences in the midst of such people as in dormitories, workshops and schools.

To the Don Bosco Salesian Coadjutor (Salesian Brother) is pointed out as a specific path to holiness in the provision of various services to the Community: Administrative and Managerial Responsibilities of particular sectors; Educational and Apostolic tasks; Missionary Evangelizing activities and a wide range of other activities. He shows the necessity and richness of their presence in the Congregation as participants in the apostolic work of the community in carrying out duties best suited to the layperson and the priest and in the possibility of bringing a Christian witness and their evangelizing work wherever it would be for the priest unsuitable or impossible to arrive.[19]

For Don Bosco, his lay Salesians were to work in the workshops and trade schools, in the office and in the city, in the classrooms, on the building site and the farm, and on the missions. In fact, in all areas where work was to be found. The Salesian Brother could fill any area of work.[20]

In our Holy Book, the Constitution of the Salesians of Francis de Sales are some articles about us as Salesians and especially the Brothers:[21]

a. Article 6 says that the Salesian vocation places us at the heart of the Church and puts us entirely at the service of her mission.

b. Article 14 says that our vocation is graced by a special gift of God: a predilection for the young.

c. Article 15 says that we are sent to the young people by the God who is 'all charity,' the Salesian is open and cordial, ready to make the first approach and to welcome others with unfailing kindliness, respect and patience.

d. And article 45 says that the Salesian Brother brings to every field of education and pastoral activity the specific qualities of his lay status, which make him in a particular way of being witness to God's Kingdom in the world, close as he is to the young and to the realities of working life. The significant and complementary presence of clerical and lay Salesians in the community constitutes an essential element of its make-up and of its apostolic completeness.

The Salesian brother is an *educator and pastor* of the young in a variety of activities – catechetical, missionary, evangelizing, educational, administrative, secretarial and domestic.

Modern society is founded on work and "the world of work" has become of great importance in many countries. For this reason, activities in the area of work are among the most important apostolic activities of the Salesian brother. Because he is close to the young and to the realities of the workers' world, his bond with young people and the world of work is a key aspect of his identity.

As an *educator*, the Salesian brother is able to face the huge challenge is in preparing young people for life in the world of work today, not only in terms of training them for their trade but especially by giving them a sound preparation for the social, ethical, spiritual and Christian challenges they will meet in life.

He inculcates in them the personal and social values that are needed in the world of work, as, for example, a spirit of brotherhood, solidarity and community, together with self-discipline and respect for every individual person. At the same time, he teaches them and helps them to overcome the evils that threaten them: a materialistic understanding of life, indifference to spiritual matters, individualism, feelings of hostility and the temptation to violence.

Moreover, through his attentive concern and constant love for them, he gives witness to a deep sense of universal brotherhood as an antidote to all forms of selfishness, exploitation and self-interest. In brief, the Salesian brother prepares young people to take their place with dignity in the Church and in society and to contribute from within to the Christian transformation of society. Don Bosco used to say: "honest citizens and good Christians."

But even though he is close to the world and secular affairs, the fact remains that he is first and foremost an *evangelizer*. He does not evangelize through priestly work – preaching, celebrating the sacraments, etc. Nor is he like a layperson outside. In fact, he works within a religious community and not in all secular affairs as the layperson outside religious life does, but only in those matters that are in keeping with the charism of the founder. He tries to act as a leaven and transform these affairs in line with the gospel.

Moreover, the consecration which derives from his religious profession confers on him the Church's mandate to proclaim the Gospel. It gives a certain quality to his work of evangelization insofar as it makes him a living witness to transcendental truths that go beyond the world: God, the kingship of Christ, the life to come, etc. His presence as a consecrated person in a secularized world is all the more urgent and precious at the present time. He reveals the kingdom of God already present in the world, in the kingship of Christ in our lives and in the values we live: love, peace, justice, etc., and the Kingdom that is to come, which we are all committed to building.

In the book of the Ratio, there is mention that the Salesian Brother "combines in himself the gifts of consecration with those of the lay state": he lives in the lay state as a consecrated person. "The presence of the Salesian Brother enriches the apostolic activity of the community. It reminds the priest members of the values inherent in the lay religious vocation and recalls to them constantly an active collaboration with laypeople. It also recalls to the Salesian priests the vision of an apostolic goal and ideal that is complex in its reality, because it goes beyond priestly and catechetical activity in the strict sense." He has a significant role to play, especially in certain contexts where the priest is seen as a sacred or cultic figure. By his consecrated life the Salesian Brother proclaims the presence of God in daily life, the importance of becoming disciples before being teachers, and bears witness to a convinced life of faith not tied to functional or ministerial duties.[22]

The writer understands that the Salesian Brother's contribution to the mission and community is the same as, of the Salesian Priest who dedicates his life to the young people who are in need. On the other hand, his mission is following the specialization for which he has prepared. So, he shares his knowledge, ability, and skill with the young people of the community to which he is sent.

The Joy of Being a Salesian Brother

The writer shares experience of three brothers:

Br. Alexander Cho23

He said that he rejoices when he meets the young people, who are able to overcome their difficult situations and stand up on their own and start an autonomous life of honest citizens.

He gave an example, in 2006 one of our youth was not able to find his life direction and spent four years in prison. He was living without any friends, so I visit him once in the prison to encourage him. After his release from prison with help of one remote relative, he was introduced to the special crane mechanics and now is living a rather good and decent life. There are many heart-moving stories of literally saving our young people from their misery, deep hurts or social marginalization. When we see them rise again for an ordinary healthy social and family life, we experience deep satisfaction, joy and happiness.

Br. Dominic Savio Wong24

In his opinion, he said can serve and help others as Salesian Brother. Whenever he serves and helps others, he happily feels that he is worthy. That is why he is always happy and joyful. Happiness is a choice. Joy is an attitude that maintains health. ... "Being happy and having a smiling face" every day is my daily motto, which reminds me that I am a happy and joyful Salesian Brother.

There are three elements that make our life of being a Salesian Brother happy and joyful: community life, mission and consecrated identity.[25]

1. The community life of fraternal life: in fraternal communities. For us Salesians, community life is a very important factor in our religious choice. In fact, for us to "live and work together" is a fundamental requirement which ensures a sure way of fulfilling our vocation. The requirement for Salesian Brother arises from the fact of our being sons of the same Father and members of the Body of Christ; religious life creates a real family made up of people who share the same faith and the same project of life. We, Salesians are called to create and to live the family spirit as Don Bosco wanted it and live it.

Our relationship ought to be fraternal and friendly, which leads us to love each other to the extent of sharing everything. This criterion helps us to see that the community is well understood and lived when it is nourished by communion and leads to communion. A communion implies with regard to acceptance, appreciation and esteem, mutual assistance and love.

GC21 situated the Salesian Brother and the Salesian Priest squarely within the Salesian community: "it will not be so much the individuals who will perpetuate his [Don Bosco's] ideals as his communities, 'formed of priests and laymen,' closely united to each other by deep brotherly ties." For this reason, the chapter went on. "the clear precise dimension of each Salesian can only be studied and evaluated adequately in the context of a brotherly and apostolic community." This chapter speaks, in fact, of the "essential mutual relationship between the Salesian Brother and the Salesian Priest."

The GC21 said that the Brother lives in constant fidelity to his specific vocation and becomes, together with his confreres, a sign of that new and permanent brotherhood established by Christ.

Mission: sent to the young. In the Constitution article 24, there is written our promise that "I offer myself totally to You. I pledge myself to devote all my strength to those to whom you will send me, especially to young people who are poorer." Then our consequence is that we shall spend less time watching TV or on other 'hobbies' and much more being available to them: to welcome them, listen to them and guide them. Then and only then, their world will become more comprehensible and we shall make our own their difficulties, their doubts, their motives, their fears, their expectations, their needs so that they can learn to listen to themselves, accept themselves, decide for themselves, in short not be simply negative or reactionary but act positively banking on those things in which they believe.

Our mission is about our identity, whether Brother or Priest is a pastor and educator of the young. This is our fundamental identity, the supreme genus, that which is common to every Salesian vocation.

The mission is not, of course, simply work. Our mission as pastors and educators consists in revealing God. We are called to be an epiphany, as was Jesus: signs and bearers of the love of God for the young, *vultus misericordiae*, those who are needed.

Consecrated identity: The Salesian mission belongs to all the members of the Salesian Family. We Salesians share in it as religious. In the light of the insistence on the sharing of our mission with the laity, the clarification and appropriation of our consecrated identity is of vital importance.

All consecrated people followed Jesus who proclaimed in word and deed the good news that our supreme vocation is communion with God. Consecrated persons are called to be precisely living memorials of Jesus, eschatological signs, in their poverty, chastity and obedience. Our life is a sign. The consecrated person is a sign through the limpidity of his life.

In a church that is not only Petrine but also Marian, Marian before being Petrine consecrated life takes its place at the Marian heart of the Church. For the Petrine ministry is destined to pass, but the Marian is the ultimate vocation of the whole church. Consecrated persons are a sign and a reminder to the whole church of its final vocation and destiny. Also, the Brother is a sign of his priest's confreres in the community. His vocation is the Salesian life in pure form, a permanent reminder to his priest confreres of their consecration.

Father Ivo quoted the letter of Pope Francis at the beginning of the year of consecrated life on 21 November 2014 that the religious follow the Lord in a special way, in a prophetic way. This is the priority that is needed right now: 'to be prophets who witness to how Jesus lived on this earth... What in particular do I expect from this Year of grace for consecrated life? That what I once said might always be true: 'Wherever there are religious, there is joy.

The writer personally has another experience that makes one happy and joyful which is praying as a community and personal prayer. Those prayers that we have: such as morning and evening prayer, Adoration, and Rosary.

These things above make our vocation as brothers happy and joyful because in community life, the mission to the young consecrated and prayer life. The writer's vocation is strengthened and supported. He does not walk alone; he is with his beloved

Salesians.

Conclusion

Vocation is a gift from God who calls all of us to create and foster relationships that will enable us to partake in the mission of the Church. In his message, Pope Benedict reminds us that "the source of every perfect gift is God who is Love." We are invited to respond freely to this gift that God himself has given us. Our response to this must be generous, free and open as we try to discern the will of God in our lives. Vocation is more than a call; it is also a mission to let others be aware of it as well. It is a mission that invites us to come, follow Christ and be "fishers of men."

There are two forms of male religious vocations: priest and lay consecrated life (brotherhood). These two expressions of the one divine love must be lived with a particular intensity and purity of heart by those who have decided to set out on the path of vocation discernment towards the ministerial priesthood and the consecrated life; they are its distinguishing mark. Love of God, which priests and consecrated persons are called to mirror, however imperfectly, is the motivation for answering the Lord's call to special consecration through priestly ordination or the profession of the evangelical counsels. Saint Peter's vehement reply to the Divine Master: 'Yes, Lord, you know that I love you (Jn 21:15) contains the secret of a life fully given and lived out, and thus one which is deeply joyful.

Our Salesian Congregation to has two forms: Priests and Brothers. It is your freedom to choose one of the two forms. Here, we talk about the Salesian Brothers' vocation. The Salesian Brother "combines in himself the gifts of consecration with those of the lay state": he lives in the lay state as a consecrated person. "The presence of Salesian Brother enriches the apostolic activity of the community. It reminds the clerical section of the values inherent in the lay religious vocation and recalls them constantly to an active collaboration with laypeople. It also recalls to the Salesian priests the vision of an apostolic goal and ideal that is complex in its reality, because it goes beyond priestly and catechetical activity in the strict sense." The Salesian Brother has a significant role to play, especially in certain contexts where the priest is seen as a sacred or cultic figure. By his consecrated life he proclaims the presence of God in daily life, and the importance of becoming disciples before being teachers, and bears witness to a convinced life of faith not tied to functional or ministerial duties.

How we can live as a Brother? It takes Self Confidence. We can proudly say, *"I am still a brother."* What is important is how I or we who are called to live our life as brothers fill our lives. If we ourselves - the brothers - are not convinced that my calling is very meaningful and worth a special way of life, which may be an attraction for those who witness our way of life. It is very disappointing when a brother is addressed or asked about the identity of his vocation, saying that I am only a brother! This answer makes the ambiguity of understanding: what a brother is. It should be answered with confidence that I am a brother! On the contrary, there are also brothers who are pretentious as priests. This appearance also confuses people's view of what is a brother. Surely this appearance is also not something that is commendable. It is necessary to realize that the call is a matter of faith. By faith, the call cannot be compared with other ways of life. Someone becomes a brother, not seek classes. It is also necessary to have confidence that a brother is called to be a brother, not to be another.

One thing that we must remember is that we should have a good intention for this vocation. in his book, Rev. Aloysius Biskupek SVD said we must have a correct understanding of good intentions, their nature, motivation, and blessings.[26] A good intention means it is an act of the will toward an end that is or is thought to be attainable. A good intention, then, implies that the object desired is good, either objectively so or at least in our own mind. A good intention, commonly understood, means the desire to glorify and please God.

Here are some questions guide for reflection and group sharing:

1. Am I happy with my vocation?
2. How do I pray the Canticle of Mary every day?

3. What kind of temptations about my vocation do I have?
4. How do I experience the wounds of sin in my heart?
5. Do I feel any excessive desire, pleasure, or freedom?
6. Do I know my temptations of selfishness?
7. Do I realize the meaning of the vows?
8. Do I pray for my personal fidelity to these commitments?
9. What has been my attitude toward vows during my life?
10. Do I think that religious men and women are really happy? Why?
11. Have I experienced friendship with a woman or with a religious sister?
12. What is my plan for the future?
13. Which aspect of Jesus' life and passion draws me deeply to Him?
14. Do I consider my vocation to the consecrated life as being linked with the Paschal Mystery and Baptism?

[16] Fr. George Williams SDB (translator), *The Project of Life of The Salesians of Don Bosco: A Guide to the Salesian Constitutions* (Madras – India, 1987), 416.

[17] *The Salesian Brother*, 27.

[18] *Project of Life*, 414.

[19] http://www.sdb.org/en/salesiani-di-don-bosco/capitoli-generali/498-cg21-1978/1280-cg-21-documento-2-1978. Taken by 20 November 2017. In Don Bosco's time the name of Salesian Brother is Salesian Coadjutor (SC).

[20] East Asia Oceania Salesian Brothers' Congress, 12.

[21] *Constitutions*, 20, 25 and 49.

[22] *Formation of Salesians of Don Bosco: Principles and Norms, Ratio Fundamentalis Institutionis et Studiorum*, Third Edition (Rome, 2009), 49-50.

[23] Taken from http://sdb.org/fr/galeries-de-photos/1466-video-missions-salesiennes.html.

[24] Br. Dominic Savio Wong, in view of the EAO Salesian Brother Congress 2018, Tainan, Taiwan, 8 December 2017 -- Br. Savio Wong is one of the senior Salesian Brothers of China province (82 years). His younger brother, Salesian priest Fr. Francis Wong just passed away in Hong Kong at the age of 74 years. Br. Savio spent most of his Salesian life in the technical school (mechanic department). At present, he is part of the dynamic Tainan community in Tainan. He took part in almost all six Salesian Brother Congresses in the history of our Region.

[25] Fr. Pascual Chavez Villanueva, acts of the General Council, Witness to the Radical Approach of the Gospel, year XCIII, Roma: 8 April 2012, No., 413, pp 33-40; and Fr Ivo Coelho, acts of the General Council, Renewed Attention to The Salesian Brother, year XCVIII (Roma: January-July 2017), No., 424., 66-75.

[26] Rev. Aloysius Biskupek, SVD. Conferences on the Religious Life (United States of America: The Bruce Publishing Company, 1960), 118-123.

CHAPTER NINE

Conclusion

This chapter will present the findings and recommendations of the project paper which aims to create a formation program, in the form of a retreat, for the Aspirantate / postulants in the initial formation.

The main objective of the project paper is to design a catechetical formation program to help young people and candidates in initial formation to know, love and eventually choose to be a religious brother, the writer assumes the main pastoral objective of the project as an attempt to design a "come and see" program. It is a three-day formation program to appreciate the vocation of the Salesian Brother in India."

In the process, the writer honestly admits the difficulty of translating the specific vocation as a brotherhood for the candidates like aspirants or postulants. This difficulty might come from the limited resources and deep knowledge that the writer had and to open the paradigm of the candidate as the people think about the brother. What is their paradigm? Their paradigm is whenever one entered the seminary he will be a priest, not a brother (only). By the way, through this course of study, the writer gained a deeper insight into the brotherhood vocation.

Besides making this project "a three-day formation program to appreciate the vocation of the Salesian Brother in India" the writer himself gain enriches about the Brotherhood vocation especially Salesian Brother. From different resources of thought, the writer gets to know better and deep than more love the vocation as Salesian Brother. To complete this section, we need to briefly answer the subquestions posed in Chapter I.

They are:

What is the religious Brother's vocation in the Church? The brother's vocation in the Church is a development of the consecration conferred by the Sacraments of Baptism and of the faith, through which he fully lives the Christian values of the People of God: sanctified and sent by God the Father for the salvation of the world, and participates in the mission and action of Christ a prophet, priest, and shepherd, and so fits in the Church's own mission to witness and proclaim the Gospel.

In the document *Lumen Gentium* (One document of The Second Vatican Council) art. 43 says that "This status of life has its place in the structure of the Ecclesiastical Hierarchy. The status of this vocation is not just a middle way between the vocation of the priest and the laity. This call is to be regarded as a special vocation for Christians, enabling them to enjoy special grace within the Church, and in each way contributing to the Church's rescue mission."[1]

What is the vocation of the Salesian Brother? As the General Chapter 21 (GC21) says that the Salesian Coadjutor (now is Salesian Brother – SB) is not an "ecclesiastic" and not merely a "layman" but SB is a baptized person called by God to give himself totally to Him in Christ, to serve him as a "lay religious" in the Salesian Congregation for young people. In it and in communion with the Salesian priest, Don Bosco creates the specific mission of promoting the integral Christian education of young people, especially the poorest.[2]

Then our congregation teaches about the Salesian brothers that the Salesian Brother "combines in himself the gifts of consecration with those of the lay state": he lives in the lay state as a consecrated person. "The presence of Salesian Brother enriches the apostolic activity of the community. It reminds the clerical section of the values inherent in the lay religious vocation and recalls them constantly to an active collaboration with laypeople. It also recalls to the Salesian priests the vision of an apostolic goal and ideal that is complex in its reality, because it goes beyond priestly and catechetical activity in the strict sense".[3]

What is the role of the Salesian Brother in the Salesian Congregation? Here are three roles that the writer could say: *first*, by his consecrated life he proclaims the presence of God in daily life, and the importance of becoming disciples before being teachers, and bears witness to a convinced life of faith not tied to functional or ministerial duties;[4] *second*, as a Salesian the Brother is first and foremost an *"educator"*, dedicated by vow to the overall advancement of the young and the common people. He carries out tasks of a cultural, professional, social and financial kind, in addition to those which are of a catechetical, liturgical and missionary in nature; in other words, he is engaged in *"every field of education and pastoral activity"*. Because, as a religious, he does not act in his own name but receives his mission from the Church, he shares deeply in the pastoral ministry, giving a particular expression to his baptismal priesthood; and *third* is by his lay condition and his experience, united with a deeply Salesian heart, make him particularly "close ... to the young and to the realities of working life". His Salesian heart is anchored in the transcendence he lives in temporal realities into which he injects the radical power of the Gospel. This enables him to move in a secular context with a mentality which is at the same time both "technical" and "pastoral", and this is of great value to the community.[5]

How can this formation program assist young people as the Salesian's candidate in initial formation to grow in knowledge and then continue their human, intellectual, spiritual and pastoral formation? First of all, the writer can say that this project paper might help the young candidate in initial formation. In "a three-day formation program to appreciate the vocation of the Salesian Brother in Indonesia" with the following topics (*The Gift of Vocation, The Gift of Vocation to Brotherhood, The Salesian Brother Vocation, Challenges and Difficulties, The Place of the Salesian Brother in the Congregation* and *The Joy of Being a Salesian Brother*) help them to understand and appreciate God's call, to understand the vocation of Salesian Brother, through deep reflection they can decide to choose to be Salesian Brother, to understand the place and role of Salesian Brother in Salesian Congregation, and to make them understand and remain faithful toward the challenge and the joy as Salesian Brothers.

They can use it to study, to know and to love the Salesian Brother vocation. Then in the end, some of them may find or discover their vocation and decide to become a Salesian Brother freely and knowingly.

RESOLUTION TO THE MAIN PASTORAL OBJECTIVE

This project book is a formation program for Aspirants and postulants in the step of initial formation to be a Salesian.

There is a proverb or saying that if one does not know then one cannot love. One needs to know a person, before being in love with that person. So, "to know" is the first step to take before loving. So, it is the case in the Brother's vocation. The writer, himself sometimes thinks and asks why many people still keep out of mind or out of their thinking about Brothers' vocation. The first reason that appears in my mind is that they do not know well who the Brothers are.

On the other hand, we can find only a few people, young people, enter the religious congregation and become a Brother. Most people choose to become priests. The writer does not think that this is a problem or struggle in Brother's vocation. In fact, there is an unknown about Brother's vocation.

To help young people and candidates in initial formation to know, love and eventually choose to be religious brothers, the writer assumes the main pastoral objective of the project as an attempt to design a "come and see" program. It is a three-day formation program to appreciate the vocation of the Salesian Brother in India." On the other hand, any conference was given by a superior (Delegation or Rector of the community) to promote the specific vocation and formation as Salesian Brother.

RECOMMENDATIONS

Given the findings and resolutions of the project paper, the following recommendations are now presented in order to further develop the catechetical formation program for aspirants and postulants as candidates for Salesian of Don Bosco.

The following are my recommendations:

For **youth ministry:** There have been many project papers written about how to do Pastoral Youth Ministry for young people. However, there appears to be lacking any formation program to train those who have applied for the religious brotherhood to be seen as youth pastoral ministers. This project paper is a response to this need and at the same time responding to the call of the Church, to have a special "program of brotherly training" which is to be undertaken by each formation house.

For Indian Delegation(in preparation to be a Vice-Province). This study will certainly help the delegate and his council in the Indian Delegation as well as the director of the candidate to rediscover the great task of formation of new candidates. In India, we have many vocations to become religious men and women. But to be religious brothers, only a few young people decide to join. This formation program might help the young people especially those young people in the initial formation to know, understand, and finally decide to become a brother knowing about this vocation.

For the young candidates in initial formation: This project paper might help the young candidate in initial formation. They can use it to study, to know and to love the Salesian Brother vocation. Then, in the end, some of them may find or discover their vocation and decide to become a Salesian Brother. So, the writer attempts this project paper to help them come to a decision freely and knowingly.

For the writer and reader: This project paper helps the writer and the reader to answer the question of where the values of brotherhood life come from. This question has always triggered his mind since the day of his first profession. The fundamental values are rooted in the biblical teaching and the life of Jesus. The understanding of these values has been in the religious life experience of the Salesian Brothers. This milieu of the Salesian Brotherhood among the confreres and the meaningful camaraderie of the Indonesian Salesian Brothers has been especially potent to appreciate the Salesian Brother's vocation.

Lastly, I recommended making the vocation of Salesian Brother more visible in the Church. There are three things we can do. *Firstly,* I think that we should pray for the Salesian Brother's vocationn. Where more vocations arise, then the more visible will the Salesian Brothers be in the Church. I cannot imagine how if there is no Salesian Brother, how the vocation could become visible in the Church. So, prayer is the first thing to do! *Second,* to strengthen and encourage those young people who decide to be Salesian Brothers by showing them the joy of Salesian life. *Third,* promoting Salesian Brother's vocation either by Salesian Brothers themselves or by Salesian Priests. The presence of the Salesian Brother in promoting his vocation influences the young people. His witness, work and duty make the young people know the Salesian Brother. The people can see the Salesian Brother face to face, contact him and be friends with them.

[1]*Ibid., Lumen Gentium,* page 403.

[2]http://www.sdb.org/en/salesiani-di-don-bosco/capitoli-generali/498-cg21-1978/1280-cg-21-documento-2-1978. Taken 20 November 2017.

[3]Formation of Salesians of Don Bosco: Principles and Norms, Rataio Fundamentalis Institutionis et Studiorum, Third Editionn, Rome, 2009., pp 49-50.

[4]*Ibid.*

[5]Fr. George Williams SDB (translator), *The Project of Life of The Salesians of Don Bosco: A Guide to the Salesian Constitutions.* Madras – India, 1987., page 416